PLANET PROBLEM SOLVERS

CREATURE CONNECTIONS

A Look at Wildlife Preservation

by Heather DiLorenzo Williams

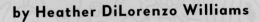

NORWOOD HOUSE PRESS

Norwood House Press

For more information about Norwood House Press please visit our website at www.norwoodhousepress.com or call 866-565-2900.
© 2023 Norwood House Press.

Credits

Editor: Mari Bolte
Designer: Sara Radka

Photo Credits Cover: ©FloridaStock/Shutterstock; page 1: ©ac productions/Getty Images; page 3: ©Dominic Cram/Getty Images; page 3: ©Vincent Pommeyrol/Getty Images; page 3: ©Edith Polverini/Getty Images; page 5: ©Nick Dolding/Getty Images; page 6: ©Jason Hosking/Getty Images; page 7: ©James HeifnerEyeEm / Getty Images; page 10: ©chuchart duangdaw/Getty Images; page 12: ©Marco Prosch/Stringer/Getty Images; page 13: ©Ed Reschke/Getty Images; page 14: ©simonkr/Getty Images; page 17: ©Mark Newman/Getty Images; page 18: ©Steve Woods Photography/Getty Images; page 19: ©THEPALMER/Getty Images; page 20: ©emanuelestano/Getty Images; page 23: ©IUCNorg; page 25: ©Mark Newman/Getty Images; page 26: ©WPA Pool/Getty Images; page 30: ©Adam Berry/Stringer/Getty Images; page 31: ©Photography by Mangiwau/Getty Images; page 33:©Buena Vista Images/Getty Images; page 36: ©SolStock/Getty Images; page 39: ©Nubefy/Shutterstock; page 41: ©GDRimages/Getty Images; page 42: ©Staff/Getty Images; page 45: ©FatCamera/Getty Images

Library of Congress Cataloging-in-Publication Data

Library of Congress Cataloging-in-Publication Data has been filed and is available at catalog.loc.gov

Hardcover ISBN: 978-1-68450-785-6
Paperback ISBN: 978-1-68404-741-3

TABLE OF CONTENTS

CHAPTER 1

WILD ABOUT WILDLIFE

Kate Gilman Williams loves animals. In 2017, she went on her first **safari** in South Africa. She was seven years old. Kate saw elephants, giraffes, and even a cheetah. Her safari guide taught her how the animals hunt or find food. She learned about their **habitats**.

But Kate also found out that some of these animals are in trouble. Many animal species are dying out in Africa and around the world. This means the number of creatures left on Earth is getting smaller and smaller. When all of one kind of animal has died out completely, it is extinct. Some of these animals are losing their habitat. Some are being hunted for fun. Some are killed for getting too close to farms and homes.

What kinds of species are endangered where you live? How did their population become threatened?

Kate decided to help when she got back home to the United States. She started a group called Kids Can Save Animals. She also co-wrote a book with her friend Michelle, her safari guide from South Africa. *Let's Go on Safari* is about Kate's experience in Africa and what she learned there. Kate wants to teach other kids about conservation and preservation. Conservation means protecting wildlife and its habitat from human activity. Preservation means keeping plants, animal life, and ecosystems natural and unchanged.

Wildlife is what lives in a certain area. Birds, fish, and insects are considered wildlife. Plants are wildlife too. You might see wildlife when you go for a walk in the woods. You can find it around a pond or near the ocean. There is even wildlife in the desert.

Animals in the wild need food and water to grow and be healthy. They need plenty of space and a safe **shelter**. They also need other animals like them. This lets them reproduce so they can keep their species alive.

Birds, Bees, Butterflies, and Bats, Oh My!

You probably know that bees help pollinate flowers. But they are not alone. Bats, butterflies, birds, and even some small mammals move pollen from plant to plant. Any animal that does this is a pollinator. When these creatures visit flowers, fruit trees, and other plants, they help more trees and plants grow. They are responsible for around one out of every three bites of food we take. But several pollinators are threatened or endangered. Without them, at least 75 percent of Earth's plants would have trouble surviving.

The plants and animals that live together in an area form an ecosystem. The rocks and land there are part of the ecosystem. The sun, water, and air are too. Everything in the ecosystem works together. Each organism and object has a job. Preserving that ecosystem means everything lives as it was intended.

Earth has many ecosystems. There are many **native** species in each one. And within a species, there are many different **genes**. This variety of living things and systems is called biodiversity. Biodiversity is important to the survival of ecosystems. And since Earth is one giant ecosystem, biodiversity is important to the health of our entire planet.

Biodiversity makes it possible for ecosystems to live and grow. Scientists check biodiversity to see how healthy Earth is. Earth can become unhealthy when there is not enough biodiversity in an area.

Humans need biodiversity for many reasons. We also get about 80 percent of our food just from plants. People use many different species of plants and animals for food. Almost half of the medicine we take comes from nature. Healthy ecosystems also give us oxygen and clean our water. Nature even gives us materials for building homes, making clothes, and creating energy.

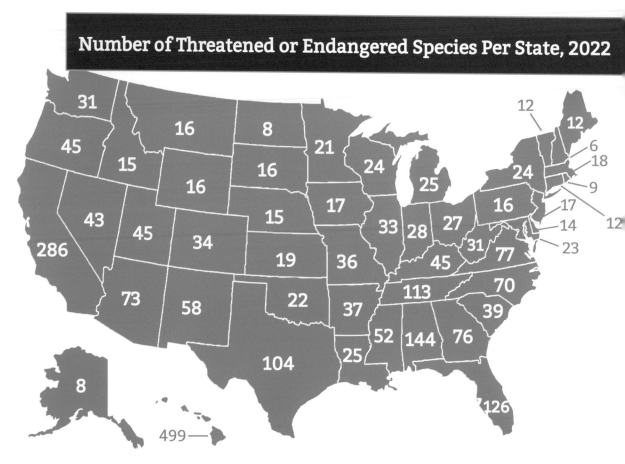

Number of Threatened or Endangered Species Per State, 2022

The Amazon rainforest is a huge ecosystem containing around 40,000 plant species, 1,300 different kinds of birds, and 2.5 million types of insects.

Since 1970, there has been a decrease in biodiversity on Earth. The world's animal population has dropped 68 percent. Biodiversity has decreased 33 percent in North America. Areas in Latin America and South America have lost 94 percent of their biodiversity. Some biodiversity loss happens naturally. But a lot of it has been caused by humans.

As Earth's temperature increases, many habitats are becoming too hot and dry for the animals that live there.

There are more people on Earth than ever before. People are responsible for most of Earth's air and water **pollution**. Pollution is a major cause of climate change. And climate change is bad news for biodiversity.

Climate change happens when Earth's temperature, weather, and atmosphere change permanently. Earth is getting hotter. Its waters are getting warmer. There is less oxygen and more **carbon dioxide** in the ocean. This disrupts the food chain for ocean animals and plants.

Pollution also **contaminates** the air and water. This harms biodiversity. There are billions of pieces of trash in the ocean. Many lakes and streams around the world contain harmful chemicals. These make it hard for ecosystems to stay healthy and balanced.

And people are not just contaminating ecosystems. They are also destroying them. Habitat destruction is another cause of biodiversity loss. Humans cut down trees and plow through fields to build houses and stores. Also, wildfires are caused by careless activities.

? Name some effects of pollution you have observed in your community. How might these be harming the ecosystems around you?

The European sturgeon was once common. But overfishing caused the species to be nearly extinct.

People also use up **resources** to get things they need. This is known as overexploitation. When there isn't enough of one species, the ecosystem is not balanced. This can mean that too many trees were cut down. It could mean too many plants or crops were picked. Sometimes, fishers catch too many fish.

Many people hunt animals for food. Sometimes, they kill more than they can eat. This is overexploitation too. Not all hunting is allowed, though. Illegal hunting is called poaching. Some hunters kill animals for fun. They use certain parts of the animals to make money. Elephant tusks are an example. They are made of ivory. And they are expensive.

Biodiversity is threatened when there is not enough of a species in an ecosystem. But sometimes there are species that don't belong there. These are called invasive species. These plants and animals are sometimes put there by humans. Sometimes, they attach to boats or crops from other places. Zebra mussels are an example. Goldfish are another. Kudzu are invasive plants. They grow quickly. They take over buildings and natural areas. Invasive species use up resources meant for the native species. This causes the ecosystem to be unbalanced.

Zebra mussels are tiny creatures native to lakes and streams in Europe and Asia that were accidentally introduced to US waters on cargo ships.

Nature provides humans with many necessary resources, including building materials for homes and other structures.

Biodiversity loss causes big problems for humans. The planet and its ecosystems are like a big web. Each of its parts are connected. If part of the web is broken, the rest is affected.

Biodiversity provides people with four services. These are provisions, regulation, support, and culture. Provisions include food, water, fuel, and supplies. Anything that can be taken from or made with something from nature is a provision.

Regulation has to do with making life possible. When something is regulated, it is made safe and usable. Plants and trees clean the air people breathe. Trees hold soil and rocks in place. Bees pollinate plants so food can grow. These are ways nature regulates life for people.

Support is what keeps living things alive. The basic cycles in nature are examples of support. These include the life cycle and the water cycle.

Culture is something that benefits people mentally and emotionally. It is how biodiversity has affected the kind of people we are.

People are part of the "web of life." We need that web to survive, but we are also causing most of its problems. Fortunately, there are many ways for people to fix some of these problems.

Name something from nature that you use or rely on every day.

CHAPTER 2

MOVING TOWARD CHANGE

The 1970s are considered the beginning of the **environmental movement**. People started caring more about the planet during this time. New laws were made about how people treat nature. This includes a law called the Endangered Species Act of 1973. Endangered means being seriously at risk of becoming extinct. The law protected animals and their habitats.

By this time, some animals were already extinct. This law helped keep us from losing more. It was part of an agreement with countries around the world to protect wildlife. Since the act was passed, 54 species in the United States have been removed from the endangered list.

Many endangered animal species were kept from becoming extinct because of the Endangered Species Act. Humpback whales, bald eagles, and gray wolves are some of them. In the 1960s, there were only around 1,000 humpback whales left in the North Pacific Ocean. They were hunted for meat and oil. Then hunting them was made illegal. Now, there are around 22,000.

The largest bald eagle populations in North America are in Alaska and Canada.

Even though laws protect them, more than 40,000 species are still in trouble. The International Union for Conservation of Nature (IUCN) keeps a list of them. It is called the IUCN Red List of Threatened Species.

A National Symbol of Success

The Founding Fathers decided in 1782 that the bald eagle would be America's national bird. They chose it because of its strength and power. Its image became an American symbol. But by the mid-1970s, there were hardly any of the birds left in the country. The eagle's power was no match for illegal hunting, habitat loss, and harmful pesticides. Several laws, including the Endangered Species Act, protected the bald eagle. Before the bird was protected, there were just 417 pairs of bald eagles. Today, there are more than 71,400 nesting pairs and 316,700 individuals. Bald eagles are no longer endangered. They are symbols not only of the US, but also of the importance of preservation.

The pelagic thresher is a species of shark that is considered endangered.

The IUCN Red List of Threatened Species has studied more than 140,000 species. Scientists made categories for the species. Some of the categories are Least Concern, Vulnerable, Endangered, and Extinct. Animals can also be Near Threatened, Critically Endangered, or Extinct in the Wild.

Scientists study the animals to figure out what their category should be. They learn about their population and habitat. They study things that might harm them or their homes. Weather patterns are studied. The ecosystem is explored.

The IUCN list helps scientists learn about biodiversity. They use it to check on Earth's health. The list also helps lawmakers. It is used to make rules about how humans treat animals and plants in the wild. Conservation groups create programs to protect wildlife based on the list. The programs are called conservation actions.

Tigers are one example of an endangered animal protected by preservation actions. All types of tigers are endangered. The tiger population is decreasing. In 1998, there were between 5,000 and 7,000. Only around 3,900 are left in the wild today. Conservation actions are helping to protect tigers. Keeping their habitats safe from harm is one action. Researching them and the things that threaten them is another.

More than 100 years ago, between 50,000 and 80,000 wild tigers lived in India. Poaching has severely reduced the number of tigers in the wild.

A healthy ecosystem includes space for animals to live, eat, hide, and play.

Conservation actions are designed for each animal on the IUCN list. Teaching people about the animal is one action. Making laws to protect the animal's habitat and food sources is another. Other laws might include making hunting the animal illegal.

Protecting and preserving the ecosystem where a species lives is important. They must have room to live, eat, and grow. They need a place to hide from **predators**. They need other animals of their kind to socialize with. Both plants and animals need others like them to reproduce. This helps the species population grow.

If a plant or animal's habitat is too crowded, there won't be enough resources for them. This means there is not enough food to go around. It means there is not enough shelter for the whole population. There might not be enough water to drink. When this happens, a species could die out. They might go somewhere else searching for a good home.

There are laws to protect certain places to keep this from happening. In the US, there are more than 40,000 protected areas. Many other places around the world are protected. Some of these places are protected to keep wildlife safe.

What are some rules at your local park, beach, or river that protect a particular animal or habitat?

Types of Protected Areas

Category	Description	% by Number	% by Area
Ia	strict nature reserve: protected area (PA) managed mainly for science	4.9	5.4
Ib	wilderness area: PA managed mainly for wilderness protection	1.2	3.3
II	national park: PA managed mainly for ecosystem protection & recreation	3.5	23.1
III	natural monument: PA managed mainly for conservation of specific natural features	17.3	1.4
IV	habitat/species management area: PA managed mainly for conservation through management intervention	24	15.5
V	protected landscape/seascape: PA managed mainly for landscape/ seascape conservation and recreation	7.4	12.4
VI	managed resource PA: PA managed mainly for the sustainable use of natural ecosystems	3.7	22.1

There are seven types of protected wildlife areas in the world. Strict Nature Reserve, Habitat/Species Management Area, and National Park are some examples. Human activity is limited in these areas. In some areas, humans cannot enter at all. In others, humans are there to do research. It is their job to make sure the wildlife is safe. Some are places humans can visit to enjoy nature and wildlife.

In the US, there are 568 wildlife **refuge** areas. Some of these areas are open to the public. But some are not. This is to protect the animals and habitats there. People may disrupt the wildlife with their presence.

There are also rescue and recovery programs for specific animals. These programs help to increase an animal's population. Some have captive breeding programs. This means scientists catch some of the animals. They keep them in natural habitats with other animals like them. The animals breed and have babies. Over time, some of the animals are released into the wild.

The red wolf is the most endangered wolf in the world. The only wild red wolves left are in North Carolina. Scientists think there are between 15 and 17 in the wild. There have been no known pups born since 2019. But there are 241 red wolves in 45 recovery centers across the US. Some have been released back into the wild.

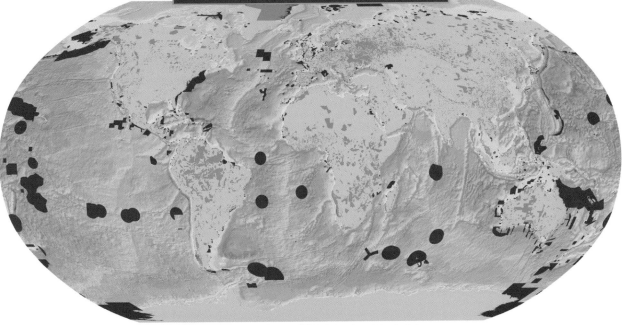

Protected Areas of the World

Terrestrial protected areas   Marine and coastal protected areas

Some animal rescue and recovery centers are found in zoos and aquariums. The Red Wolf Recovery Program works with zoos across the US. One is the North Carolina Zoological Park. Three litters of red wolf puppies were born there in 2021. The zoo's wolf pack has 36 wolves. Because of programs like this, the red wolf is not extinct.

Another animal that has been saved from extinction is the California condor. This is a species of vulture. It is the largest wild bird in North America. The California condor was the first animal to be put on the endangered species list in 1973. In 1987, there were only 27 of them left. Scientists captured all 27 birds. They put them in zoos where they were safe. Natural habitats and breeding programs helped the condor population grow.

There are now around 329 California condors living in the wild again. Another 175 live in zoos across America. The bird is still critically endangered. But recovery programs, zoos, and conservation groups saved it from becoming extinct.

What are some threatened or endangered animals that you have seen in a local zoo or science center?

Captive breeding programs like the one at the North Carolina Zoological Park are helping to make sure that the red wolf does not become extinct.

The United Kingdom's Prince Charles is one of many public figures who support the World Wildlife Foundation.

There are many conservation and preservation groups in the US and around the world. They work with the government to make laws that protect wildlife. They teach people about the importance of biodiversity. These groups also raise money to help protect wildlife.

The World Wildlife Fund (WWF) is one of the best-known groups. It works with people all over the world. The WWF raises money to fund conservation projects. The group has worked to save tigers and rhinos. It has also helped make several rainforests into protected preserves.

The Nature Conservancy is another group. It is based in the US. The Nature Conservancy focuses on protecting land and water in the US and around the world. They have protected more than 125 million acres (50.6 million hectares) of land.

The National Wildlife Federation (NWF) is also based in the US. The NWF wants to protect wild animal populations across America. The group restores damaged habitats. They help protect the places where animals live and eat.

Thanks to conservation and preservation groups and special programs, many people are working to protect the world's biodiversity. But there is still a long way to go. And there are many ways for people to help.

CHAPTER 3

WILD INNOVATIONS

Scientists think there are around 8.7 million species of plants and animals on Earth. They have only identified 1.6 million of them. The WWF and the Zoological Society of London study just 4,000 of those species to better understand biodiversity. The Living Planet **database** is the result of their work.

The Living Planet database combines **data** gathered from thousands of sources around the world. Data is information. It comes in many forms. Data could be a recording of lions roaring. It could be a photograph of an injured elephant. Data includes numbers of an animal species living in a place. It includes descriptions of habitats. Human and natural threats are part of this data too.

Data on species populations comes from thousands of sources around the world. Audio devices measure animal sounds. Drones take photos and videos from the air. Satellites in space use **GPS tags** to track animals.

Scientists believe they have only discovered one-third of the creatures that live in the world's oceans.

The Living Planet database collects all of this data. Anyone can create an account and access it. Scientists look at which animals are in trouble. They also look at which animals are healthy and thriving. Scientists work with the WWF and other programs. They use the information to improve biodiversity around the world. Being able to see change over time can show risks and rewards.

Many scientists are using satellites to collect data. Satellites take pictures of Earth every day. These pictures show how a place changes over time. A tool from Google called Earth Engine lets people search for an exact location. All the satellite images from that place can be viewed at once. Scientists can look at tree growth or loss. They can see a change in water levels in the ocean. They can see changes in ice and snow.

Satellite photos of Earth taken over time give researchers a better idea of how the planet is changing.

How can observing one area over a long period of time help scientists understand changes?

About 80 percent of land animals and plants live in forests. Cutting down too many trees is a threat to their safety.

Using Earth Engine helps scientists figure out where wildlife might be threatened. It helps them see where animal habitats need help. Having this data helps scientists and conservation groups when they talk to people who make laws. They can show how important it is to protect natural areas. They can explain why we need to get rid of pollution.

A group of scientists in Minnesota used Earth Engine to study wild tiger habitats in Asia. They looked at pictures taken over 14 years. The scientists learned how much forest had been lost. They discovered that if forest loss ended, the wild tiger habitat could be doubled in just a few years.

People who work to protect wildlife also use drones. These remote-controlled aircraft do not disturb animals as much as a plane or helicopter might. Drones are small and do not make too much noise.

Drones allow scientists to get close to groups of animals safely. People have used them to track many different animals, from bison to sharks. They can get close to animals who live on cliffs or deep in forests. Animals who might get scared by humans, like herds of deer or schools of fish, don't mind a drone.

Photos and video taken with drones can show how many animals are in an area. They can show if animals are injured or sick. Audio recordings from drones help scientists learn how animals communicate. Special cameras allow them to record even at night.

Drones can get into spaces that people can't get to. They can show damage from fires or **drought**. Drones can help measure habitat loss. Some groups have used drones to plant trees. They can even help officials track poachers.

Scientists have also used **artificial intelligence** (AI) software to prevent poaching. The software uses data of past poaching incidents. It uses locations of traps that have been found. Then, it predicts where poachers might go next. Rangers and authorities can go and stop them.

Drones can allow researchers to get much closer to animals in the wild than they could in a car or on foot.

Peccaries are small rainforest-dwelling pigs that help spread seeds and create habitats for smaller species.

Robots are also being used to monitor and protect animals. Some are similar to drones. They can go underwater or on the ground. Many are small and don't make much noise. They blend in and do not disturb animals. These robots record sounds and videos. They take pictures. Some can even take blood samples from animals. They are so small that the animal does not even notice. Scientists can use these samples to check the health of animals in the wild.

Scientists have also created a tiny robot tracking tag. These have been used on huge humpback whales in the ocean and small pigs called peccaries in the Amazon rainforest. The tags allow scientists to study each species. But they also help the animals avoid danger and find food. The pigs' tags vibrate and guide them to safe areas. Scientists can use underwater speakers on the whales' tags to let them know when they are too close to a ship.

Other robots are made to look like animals. Robotic fish and manta rays swim in parts of the ocean. They do not disturb the other fish. Built-in sensors study the effects of climate change on **reefs**. They monitor water temperature and changes in the water. They check on the health of marine life. Tiny underwater cameras take pictures and videos of the reefs and the fish who live around them. Scientists use video game controls to move the robotic fish around in the water.

Conservation Goes to the Dogs

Many groups are using technology to solve problems in nature. But some are relying on man's best friend. A dog's sense of smell is thousands of times better than a person's. Around the globe, dogs are helping conservationists sniff out invasive species. They are tracking rare plants and endangered species. Some are even helping law enforcement find and catch poachers. Many of the dogs are rescued from shelters. Not only are they getting a second chance, but they are also helping people save the planet one sniff at a time.

You don't have to be a trained scientist to collect wildlife data. The public helps solve real-world problems with everyday tools. Smartphones and digital cameras allow ordinary people to help protect biodiversity. This is called citizen science.

Citizen scientists are volunteers. This means they do not get paid to help with research. But the data they collect is important. Scientists and researchers can't be everywhere. They might need to collect data about frogs from locations all over North America. Citizen scientists can help.

A program called FrogWatch USA studies wetlands all over the country. Frogs and toads help scientists understand how climate changes are affecting ecosystems. Volunteers can visit ponds and streams near them. They can use their smartphones to collect data. Anyone can help. Families, groups, and classes can be a part of the program.

There are citizen science programs for birds, butterflies, and bees too. There are programs that help monitor sea turtles. There are programs for plants and trees. Citizen scientists can even help track pollution and weather. Everyone can help solve Earth's biodiversity problem.

What is something you can do with your family to help wild animals who live nearby?

All of this data is important. Proof that animals and ecosystems are in trouble is the first step to solving the problem. Scientists and conservation groups share data with people in charge of laws and regulations. They share information with people who are in charge of land. Groups also use data to find patterns and figure out solutions. They share information with people who volunteer and donate money.

Giving money is one way to help with wildlife conservation and land preservation. Groups use donations to buy new technology. They pay scientists who study and research animals. Projects to protect animals in the wild cost money too. Every penny helps. You can organize a fundraiser with your friends or class. Maybe there is a wildlife program in your area! But there are lots of other ways to help too.

Families who want to help protect wildlife can write letters to politicians. State and federal officials vote on laws. Many laws affect the environment. It is important to tell them why they should care about animals and their homes. Letters from voters can help them decide on issues. If officials hear from many people, they are more likely to help. Climate change, illegal hunting, and protecting endangered species are some important issues.

10 Actions You Can Take to Conserve Endangered Species

1. **Volunteer** with endangered species conservation organizations.
2. **Reduce** your carbon footprint. Use less plastic. Walk and bike. Take the bus. Eat less meat. Advocate for climate change education and carbon reduction policies.
3. **Protect** ecosystems and habitats: support laws creating open space, wildlife crossings and corridors, and other protections.
4. **Report** harassment and cruelty toward animals.
5. **Garden** without pesticides and herbicides: toxic chemicals can migrate up the food chain, harming and killing a range of species.
6. **Plant** native plant species: cultivate native, regionally appropriate plant species, creating a habitat for pollinators and other species.
7. **Never** buy products made from threatened/endangered animals or live animals and plants. Help end illegal species trade.
8. **Travel** compassionately: don't participate in activities that exploit threatened/endangered species, such as animal selfies, animal rides, or trophy hunting.
9. **Choose** alternatives to single-use plastic: reuseable bags, utensils, straws, and packaging. Advocate for increased recycling and measures like plastic bag bans.
10. **Raise** your voice to support threatened and endangered species. Vote for elected officials, and attend city and county council and game agency meetings. Share information about issues. Email, tweet, or call your member of Congress. Create and sign petitions. Write letters to the editor.

There are lots of things families can do at home too. Making less waste is one way we can help wildlife. Families who recycle and compost don't have as much trash. Recycling makes plastic, glass, and other waste into new things. Composting turns food and yard waste into fertilizer. Both of these are good for the environment.

Preserving animals' habitats is an important way to conserve wildlife. Keeping trash out of natural places keeps those spaces safe for plants and animals. Animals sometimes mistake trash for food. Trash also causes pollution. Keeping pollution out of the air and water helps keep Earth and its wildlife healthy. Remember to keep trash cans around your house sealed so wildlife can't get into them. Always clean up after a hike or picnic. You can even hold a stream or beach cleanup.

Supporting native plants and animals can help keep invasive species away. Plant native flowers and herbs in your yard. Flowers native to your area attract bees. If you go fishing or visit a stream, make sure you don't bring plants or bugs back to your yard. And never release a fish or critter from a pet store into the wild. These creatures can take food and other resources from native animals.

You can even become a citizen scientist. Look for a project in your area. Citizen scientists can be any age!

Healthy native plants and flowers attract native animals. They work together to create biodiversity.

Even though many animals are protected, thousands are still in trouble. Many groups are trying to help them. Scientists are doing research. Inventors are using technology. Conservation groups are teaching people about endangered species.

Learning about threatened or endangered animals is something everyone can do. Finding out more about animals and places that are in trouble makes people care more about them. When you know more about endangered animals, you understand how their lives affect yours. You can check out a book or visit a local zoo or science center. Maybe you can even go on a safari like Kate Gilman Williams!

Visiting animals in the wild inspired Kate. Her conservation group encourages other kids to help save endangered species. And there are many who are doing just that!

Will Gladstone, age 16, and his brother Matthew, age 13, started the Blue Feet Foundation. The boys sell bright blue socks on their website. They have raised more than $150,000 to help save the blue-footed booby, an endangered bird.

Seventeen-year-old Teagan Yardley makes movies about endangered wildlife. Her films teach and inspire people. In 2019, she won an international award for her work in conservation.

Teagan, Will, Matthew, and Kate are proof that kids of all ages can help with wildlife conservation. They are learning about ecosystems, climate change, biodiversity, and endangered species. Then, they are taking what they learn and changing the world—and so can you!

Activity 1:

Design, draw, color, and label a wildlife-friendly habitat that might be found in your city or community.

MATERIALS:

- access to the internet
- paper
- colored pencils or markers

PROCEDURE

1. Research native plants, insects, birds, and animals in your area. Learn about native flowers and their natural pollinators. Find out what kinds of birds live in your trees. Gather facts about frogs, turtles, squirrels, and other critters that live nearby.

2. Design a garden habitat. Pick some native plants and flowers. Select items such as bird feeders or fountains that might attract native creatures.

3. Draw and label each item in your garden habitat.

4. If you have time and resources, you could even get your family to help you make your drawing a reality!

Activity 2:

Participate in a citizen science project with your class. Research projects online and find one that's nearby, or one that you can do from anywhere.

MATERIALS:

- access to the internet
- other items based on the project selected

PROCEDURE:

1. With help from your teacher or media specialist, research citizen science projects in your area. A great place to start is https://www.nationalgeographic.org/idea/citizen-science-projects.

2. Sign up for one as a class. Then, start helping save the planet!

GLOSSARY

ARTIFICIAL INTELLIGENCE (ar-tuh-fish-UHL in-TELL-uh-junz): a machine that has the ability to think like a person

CARBON DIOXIDE (KAR-buhn die-OKS-eyed): a colorless, odorless gas; animals and humans breathe it out, and plants use it to make food

CONTAMINATES (con-TAM-uh-nayts): to make dirty or poisonous

DATA (DAY-tuh): information

DATABASE (DAY-tuh-bays): a collection of information stored in a computer

DROUGHT (DROWT): when land is too dry because of too little rain

ENVIRONMENTAL MOVEMENT (en-vy-ruh-MEN-tuhl MOOV-muhnt): a worldwide effort involving multiple people, activist groups, and government organizations to address issues related to nature and the health of the planet

GENES (JEENZ): tiny parts of a cell that determine the characteristics of an organism

GPS TAGS (GEE-PEE-ESS TAGZ): tiny devices that track the location of an item, animal, or person using satellites

HABITATS (HAB-uh-tats): the natural homes of a plant or animal

NATIVE (NAY-tiv): growing or living naturally in a particular place

POLLUTION (puh-LOO-shuhn): items or chemicals that harm Earth's water, air, and land

PREDATORS (PRED-uh-tuhrs): animals that hunt other animals for food

REEFS (REEFS): underwater strips of rocks, coral, or sand near the surface of the ocean

REFUGE (REF-yooj): a place that provides protection

RESOURCES (REE-soar-suhz): materials that are useful or valuable

SAFARI (suh-FAHR-ee): a trip to view animals in their natural homes, usually in Africa

SHELTER (SHEL-tuhr): a safe, covered place

FOR MORE INFORMATION

BOOKS

Alex, David. *Dying Off: Endangered Plants and Animals.* New York, NY: Cavendish Square, 2020.

Clarke, Ginjer L. *The Fascinating Animal Book for Kids: 500 Wild Facts!* Emeryville, CA: Rockridge Press, 2021.

Idzikowski, Lisa. *Biodiversity and Conservation.* New York, NY: Greenhaven Publishing, 2020.

WEBSITES

Biodiversity—Everything Counts!

https://www.amnh.org/explore/ology/biodiversity
This site is filled with fun facts, kid-friendly articles, and biodiversity activities.

How to Save the Planet: A Guide for Kids

https://www.natgeokids.com/uk/discover/science/nature/how-to-save-the-planet/
A family-friendly guide to nature conservation that includes statistics, fun facts, and useful strategies.

Kids Can Save Animals

https://kidscansaveanimals.com/
Informative site that includes a wealth of information about endangered species, as well as easy ways kids can get involved in conservation.

INDEX

ABOUT THE AUTHOR

Heather DiLorenzo Williams is a writer and educator with a passion for seeing readers of all ages connect with others through stories and personal experiences. She enjoys running, reading, and watching sports. Heather lives in North Carolina with her husband and two children.